Celestial Cannabis

Celestial Cannabis

A ZODIAC JOURNEY

Matthew Petchinsky

Apophis Enterprises LLC

1

Celestial Cannabis: A Zodiac Journey

<u>Celestial Cannabis: A Zodiac Journey</u>
By: Matthew Petchinsky

<u>**Introduction 1A**</u>

Astrology has been a fascination for thousands of years, there are many different versions of it and it has had the hearts and mind of man in every culture on Earth, since mankind was primitive Caveman in a cave to Egyptian to modern man. Astrology is engrained in our DNA. Please enjoy this book.

Introduction: Aligning the Stars with the Strains

The Cosmic Connection

In the expansive tapestry of the universe, where stars dictate destinies and plants hold ancient wisdom, there lies a unique intersection between the celestial and the terrestrial: the harmonious blend of astrology and cannabis. This connection, both profound and personal, offers a path to understanding oneself through the mirror of the cosmos, guided by the stars and supported by the Earth. Astrology, the ancient art of interpreting the movements and positions of celestial bodies, offers insights into character, emotions, and potential futures. Cannabis, with its myriad strains and effects, provides a versatile tool for healing, exploration, and personal growth. Together, they form a synergy that can lead to profound discoveries and experiences.

The intertwining paths of astrology and cannabis are not a recent phenomenon but are rooted in centuries of tradition, where shamans and healers looked to the stars for guidance and to plants for healing. In this modern reimagining, we explore how the qualities of different cannabis strains can complement the energetic influences of the zodiac signs, enhancing self-awareness, healing, and spiritual growth. This celestial pairing encourages a journey of self-discovery, where the cosmic influences of your zodiac sign can guide you to the cannabis strains that resonate most deeply with your spiritual, emotional, and physical needs.

Navigating the Zodiac Journey

"Celestial Cannabis: A Zodiac Journey" is designed to be a companion guide on your exploration of self through the dual lenses of astrology and cannabis. Whether you are a seasoned astrologer, a cannabis connoisseur, or new to either world, this book offers a structured yet intuitive path to understanding how these elements interconnect. Each chapter is dedicated to a specific zodiac sign, detailing its characteristics, challenges, and strengths, and pairing these with complementary cannabis strains that enhance or balance these qualities.

To navigate this journey, begin by finding your Sun sign chapter, which reflects your core identity, and explore the cannabis strains aligned with your sign's energy. Don't stop there—consider also your Moon sign, which represents your emotional and inner self, and your Ascendant or Rising sign, which illustrates how you present yourself to the world. By exploring the cannabis strains associated with these aspects of your chart, you can embark on a well-rounded journey of self-exploration and cosmic alignment.

Understanding Cannabis

Before delving into the zodiac journey, it's essential to lay the groundwork with a basic understanding of cannabis. Cannabis strains are broadly categorized into three types: Indica, known for its relaxing and sedative effects; Sativa, recognized for its energizing and uplifting effects; and Hybrid, which blends characteristics of both Indica and Sativa. Each strain possesses a unique profile of terpenes and cannabinoids that contribute to its effects, flavors, and aromas.

The experience of consuming cannabis is subjective and influenced by individual biology, mindset, and setting. Therefore, intention plays a crucial role in the consumption of cannabis, especially when embarking on a journey of self-discovery and spiritual growth. By setting intentions, such as seeking relaxation, enhancing creativity, or promoting introspection, you can align your cannabis consumption with your personal and astrological exploration.

As you journey through "Celestial Cannabis: A Zodiac Journey," keep an open mind and heart. Allow the cosmic wisdom of the stars to guide you, and let the ancient plant ally of cannabis support your path to self-understanding and cosmic alignment.

Chapter 1: Aries – The Fiery Sativa Surge

Characteristics of Aries

Aries, the first sign of the zodiac, embodies the vigor and vitality of new beginnings. Born between March 21st and April 19th, Aries individuals are pioneers at heart, characterized by their dynamic energy, boldness, and innate leadership qualities. Governed by Mars, the planet of action and desire, Aries exudes confidence and prefers to lead rather than follow. Their fire element bestows upon them an enthusiastic and sometimes impulsive nature, driven by a passion for discovery and an eagerness to face challenges head-on.

In the celestial dance of astrology and cannabis, Aries' traits align closely with the stimulating and uplifting qualities of Sativa strains. Just as Aries individuals are known for their boundless energy and fearless spirit, Sativa strains offer an energetic surge that can enhance focus, creativity, and motivation. This alignment offers Aries a unique opportunity to harness the power of cannabis to amplify their natural strengths and address their challenges, such as impatience or a tendency towards frustration when faced with delays or obstacles.

Recommended Strains for Aries

For the Aries seeking to match their fiery spirit with an equally invigorating cannabis experience, here are some energetic Sativa strains that are particularly well-suited to this zodiac sign:

1. **Green Crack:** Known for its sharp energy and focus, Green Crack is the perfect ally for Aries tackling a busy day full of challenges. This strain delivers a mental buzz that can enhance Aries' natural

leadership and problem-solving abilities, making it easier to navigate obstacles with confidence.

2. **Sour Diesel**: With its fast-acting effects that produce dreamy cerebral energy, Sour Diesel is ideal for Aries looking to fuel their adventurous side. This strain can ignite creativity and propel Aries into action, perfect for brainstorming sessions or embarking on new projects.

3. **Jack Herer**: Named after the cannabis activist, Jack Herer offers a blissful, clear-headed, and creative experience. This strain is a fantastic choice for Aries seeking to channel their energy into creative endeavors or to inspire leadership and initiative in social movements.

4. **Super Silver Haze**: For the Aries seeking a balance between mental stimulation and physical relaxation, Super Silver Haze provides an energetic high that's grounded by a subtle body buzz. This strain can help Aries individuals maintain their stamina and focus during long endeavors without burning out.

Cannabis Rituals for Aries

To fully embrace the fiery energy of Aries and the stimulating effects of Sativa strains, incorporating tailored cannabis rituals can enhance ambition, initiative, and the pursuit of goals. Here are some rituals designed specifically for Aries:

1. **Morning Motivation Ritual**: Begin your day by setting intentions and meditating with a Sativa strain like Green Crack. Use this time to focus on your goals and the actions required to achieve them. The energetic surge from the cannabis will align with your natural morning vigor, setting a powerful tone for the day.

2. **Creative Flow Session**: Aries is known for their creative and innovative spirit. Engage in a creative flow session by consuming a strain like Jack Herer before diving into your creative work. Whether it's writing, painting, or brainstorming, allow the cannabis to amplify your natural creativity and drive.

3. **Adventure and Exploration**: Embrace your adventurous side by planning an outdoor activity or a new experience while enjoying Sour Diesel. Whether it's hiking, biking, or exploring a new place, the energizing effects of the strain will enhance your sense of adventure and discovery.

4. **Reflective Journaling**: At the end of the day, wind down with a slightly more balanced strain like Super Silver Haze and engage in reflective journaling. Reflect on your achievements, the challenges you faced, and how you can align your actions more closely with your goals. This practice can help Aries individuals to harness their energy effectively and maintain focus on their long-term ambitions.

By aligning the fiery spirit of Aries with the energetic surge of Sativa strains, "Celestial Cannabis: A Zodiac Journey" invites Aries individuals to explore the synergy between their astrological identity and cannabis. Through tailored strains and rituals, Aries can amplify their natural strengths, navigate their challenges, and embark on a journey of self-discovery and cosmic alignment.

If you want to see some amazing products, please visit my Virtual Dispensary: https://shift.store/sg1fan23477/retail

Chapter 2: Taurus – Earthy Indica Grounding

Characteristics of Taurus

Taurus, the steadfast builder of the zodiac, enjoys the sensual pleasures of life like no other sign. Born between April 20th and May 20th, Taureans are defined by their earthy, grounded nature, exuding calmness, reliability, and a profound connection to the physical world. Ruled by Venus, the planet of love, beauty, and money, Taureans have an innate appreciation for the finer things in life, from gourmet food to luxurious comforts. Their steadfast and sometimes stubborn nature is a testament to their deep need for stability and consistency.

The essence of Taurus resonates with the soothing and grounding effects of Indica strains. Just as Taurus seeks comfort, relaxation, and enjoyment in the sensory world, Indica strains offer a calming experience, reducing stress and enhancing physical sensations. This alignment allows Taureans to deepen their connection to their senses, indulge in relaxation, and reinforce their natural affinity for beauty and pleasure.

Recommended Strains for Taurus

For Taurus, the ideal cannabis strains are those that embody richness, depth, and the capacity to enhance sensory experiences. Here are some recommended Indica strains that align with Taurus' earthy and sensual nature:

1. **Granddaddy Purple**: Known for its dreamy bliss and ability to relax the body, Granddaddy Purple is perfect for Taurus individuals looking to unwind and indulge in their love for comfort. Its grape and berry aromas also appeal to Taureans' appreciation for fine tastes and scents.

2. **Northern Lights**: This classic strain offers profound relaxation and a sense of peace, ideal for the Taurus seeking to de-stress and enjoy a quiet night in. Northern Lights helps ground Taureans, connecting them deeper to their earthy roots.

3. **Blue Cheese**: With its unique blend of flavors and deeply relaxing effects, Blue Cheese is suited for Taurus' love of the unique and

luxurious. This strain can enhance the sensory experience, making every touch, taste, and smell even more pleasurable.

4. **Afghan Kush**: Originating from the Hindu Kush mountain range, Afghan Kush is a pure Indica strain known for its heavy, body-focused effects. It's perfect for Taurus individuals seeking deep relaxation and a mental escape into their own sensory world.

Cannabis Rituals for Taurus

Taurus individuals can enhance their connection to the earth and indulge in their sensual nature through tailored cannabis rituals. Here are some practices designed to align with Taurus' love for relaxation, beauty, and sensual pleasure:

1. **Sensory Exploration Ritual**: Taurus is all about the senses. Create a ritual around consuming a strain like Blue Cheese or Granddaddy Purple, then engage in activities that heighten your sensory perception. This could be tasting a variety of fine chocolates, listening to high-fidelity music, or enjoying the texture of luxurious fabrics.

2. **Nature Connection Ritual**: As an earth sign, Taurus has a deep connection to nature. Enjoy a session with Afghan Kush or Northern Lights before spending time in nature, whether it's a leisurely walk in the forest, gardening, or simply sitting under a tree. Allow the calming effects of the Indica to enhance your feeling of groundedness and connection to the earth.

3. **Artistic Appreciation Ritual**: With Venus as their ruling planet, Taureans naturally appreciate beauty and art. Use a strain like Granddaddy Purple to relax and open your senses, then visit an art gallery, museum, or engage in your own artistic creation. The cannabis will enhance your appreciation of color, form, and beauty, deepening the experience.

4. **Luxury Bath Ritual**: Indulge in a luxury bath ritual by incorporating a soothing strain like Northern Lights. Set the scene with scented candles, bath bombs, and soft music to create a spa-like atmosphere. The Indica's relaxing properties will help soothe your

muscles and calm your mind, allowing you to fully immerse in the sensual pleasure of the experience.

Through these recommended strains and rituals, Taurus individuals can deepen their connection to their sensual nature, find relaxation and grounding, and further cultivate their appreciation for beauty. "Celestial Cannabis: A Zodiac Journey" invites Taureans to explore the earthy comforts and pleasures that cannabis can bring to their lives, aligning their celestial qualities with the grounding force of Indica strains.

If you want to see some amazing products, please visit my Virtual Dispensary: https://shift.store/sg1fan23477/retail

Chapter 3: Gemini – The Hybrid Twins

Characteristics of Gemini

Gemini, symbolized by the Twins, is the zodiac sign that embodies duality, versatility, and a vibrant flow of energy that seems to be ever-changing. Born between May 21st and June 20th, Geminis are known for their quick wit, intellectual curiosity, and innate ability to adapt to different situations with ease. Ruled by Mercury, the planet of communication, Geminis thrive in social settings, displaying a remarkable ability to converse and exchange ideas. Their air element endows them with an insatiable thirst for knowledge, new experiences, and connections with people.

The dual nature of Gemini resonates well with the balanced effects of Hybrid cannabis strains, which combine the uplifting cerebral high of Sativas with the relaxing body effects of Indicas. This synergy offers Geminis the best of both worlds, catering to their multifaceted personalities and supporting their dynamic lifestyles. Hybrid strains can enhance Gemini's social nature, stimulate their creativity, and provide relaxation when they need to wind down.

Recommended Strains for Gemini

To complement Gemini's love for variety and their adaptable nature, here are some Hybrid strains that offer a nuanced balance of effects:

1. **Blue Dream**: This popular Hybrid offers a perfect balance between cerebral stimulation and physical relaxation. Blue Dream is ideal for Geminis looking to spark their creativity, engage in philosophical discussions, or simply enjoy a pleasant, balanced high.

2. **Pineapple Express**: Known for its energizing and mood-lifting effects, Pineapple Express is a great choice for Geminis engaging in social activities or creative projects. Its ability to enhance mental clarity while also providing a gentle body buzz aligns well with Gemini's dynamic energy.

3. **Gelato**: For Geminis seeking a more pronounced euphoria that

doesn't compromise their ability to socialize and stay active, Gelato offers a potent yet balanced high. Its delicious flavor profile also appeals to Gemini's appreciation for variety and novelty.

4. **White Widow**: A classic Hybrid, White Widow stimulates the mind while offering a comfortable, soothing body high. It's particularly suited for Geminis who love to delve into deep conversations or immerse themselves in reading and writing, as it enhances focus and creativity.

Cannabis Rituals for Gemini

Gemini's versatile nature and love for social interaction can be further enhanced through specific cannabis rituals designed to stimulate conversation, creativity, and connections:

1. **Social Creativity Session**: Organize a get-together with friends where everyone partakes in a strain like Blue Dream. Combine it with activities that engage the mind and promote creativity, such as painting, brainstorming business ideas, or playing music. This ritual is perfect for stimulating Gemini's intellectual curiosity and love for social gatherings.

2. **Mindful Movement**: Gemini's air element makes them crave movement and mental engagement. A session with Pineapple Express followed by a group yoga class, dance, or a light hike can satisfy their need for physical activity while keeping the mind sharp and engaged.

3. **Book Club with a Twist**: Geminis love to learn and exchange ideas. Starting a book club where discussions are paired with a specific cannabis strain, like Gelato, can offer a new layer of depth to conversations and insights, making the experience more engaging and multifaceted.

4. **Travel or Explore Locally**: Geminis have a natural urge to explore and experience new things. A day trip to a new city or a hidden gem in their own town, enhanced by a strain like White Widow, can make the adventure more vivid and memorable. The cannabis

can heighten their senses, making every sight, sound, and taste an integral part of the journey.

Through these recommended strains and rituals, Geminis can embrace their dual nature, enjoying the balanced harmony that Hybrid strains provide. "Celestial Cannabis: A Zodiac Journey" invites Gemini individuals to explore the dynamic interplay of cerebral and physical experiences, enriching their endless quest for knowledge, creativity, and social connection with the versatile magic of cannabis.

If you want to see some amazing products, please visit my Virtual Dispensary: https://shift.store/sg1fan23477/retail

Chapter 4: Cancer – Comforting Indica Waters

Characteristics of Cancer

Cancer, the sign of the Crab, is the heart of the zodiac, known for its deep emotional currents, nurturing instincts, and a profound connection to home and family. Born between June 21st and July 22nd, Cancerians are intuitive, sensitive, and possess a strong protective streak for those they hold dear. Governed by the Moon, which represents emotions and inner life, Cancer's moods and feelings flow and change like the lunar phases. This water sign craves emotional security and comfort, often acting as the emotional anchor in their relationships.

Cancer's emotional depth and need for comfort find solace in the soothing embrace of Indica strains and CBD-rich options. These varieties offer a calming effect, helping to ease stress, alleviate anxiety, and provide a sense of physical and emotional well-being. The gentle support of these strains can help Cancerians navigate their inner emotional seas, offering a comforting lighthouse amidst the waves.

Recommended Strains for Cancer

For Cancerians seeking emotional and physical comfort, the following Indica and CBD-rich strains can offer solace and support:

1. **Grandma's Boy**: This Indica-dominant strain is known for its calming effects, making it perfect for Cancerians looking to unwind and find peace in their often tumultuous emotional waters. Its soothing properties can also aid in sleep, providing restful nights.

2. **ACDC**: A CBD-rich strain, ACDC can offer relief without a strong psychoactive high, making it ideal for Cancerians who are more sensitive to THC's effects. It's particularly well-suited for managing anxiety, pain, and stress, providing a gentle buffer to the world's harshness.

3. **Northern Lights**: Famous for its ability to relax the mind and body, Northern Lights is a go-to for emotional comfort. It can help

Cancerians let go of their worries and bask in the warm glow of tranquility, enhancing their innate need for security and comfort.

4. **Harlequin**: This strain stands out for its balanced CBD:THC ratio, offering both relief from physical discomfort and a mild, uplifting euphoria. Harlequin can help Cancerians maintain emotional balance, easing anxiety while encouraging positive feelings and comfort.

Cannabis Rituals for Cancer

To nurture Cancer's soul and provide a haven for emotional processing, the following cannabis rituals can offer intimate and comforting practices:

1. **Evening Unwind Ritual**: Create a sanctuary in your home where you can retreat and relax. Light some candles, play soft music, and partake in a strain like Grandma's Boy. Use this time to journal, meditate, or simply be with your thoughts, allowing the Indica's soothing properties to wash over you, providing comfort and calm.
2. **Bath Time Bliss**: Enhance your self-care routine with a cannabis-infused bath. Use CBD bath bombs or oils and immerse yourself in warm water while enjoying ACDC or Harlequin. This ritual can help soothe both body and mind, offering a nurturing space for emotional healing.
3. **Comfort Cooking**: Engage in the therapeutic act of cooking a nourishing meal for yourself or loved ones. Before starting, consume a strain like Northern Lights to enhance the sensory experience of cooking and eating. This ritual can help ground you, providing a sense of comfort and fulfillment.
4. **Moonlit Meditation**: Align with your ruling celestial body, the Moon, by meditating under its light. Choose a calming strain like Grandma's Boy to deepen your meditation practice. Reflect on your emotions, thoughts, and the constant change they embody, finding peace in the natural ebb and flow of life.

Through these recommended strains and nurturing rituals, "Celestial Cannabis: A Zodiac Journey" invites Cancerians to explore the comforting embrace of Indica and CBD-rich cannabis. This exploration can offer a supportive foundation for emotional processing, self-care, and the cultivation of inner peace, aligning Cancer's emotional depths with the soothing waters of cannabis.

If you want to see some amazing products, please visit my Virtual Dispensary: https://shift.store/sg1fan23477/retail

Chapter 5: Leo – The Sativa Spotlight

Characteristics of Leo

Leo, symbolized by the Lion, reigns with a heart full of courage, a spirit of leadership, and an undeniable charisma that draws the spotlight naturally. Born between July 23rd and August 22nd, Leos are known for their boldness, warmth, and a generous penchant for drama and flair. Ruled by the Sun, the center of our solar system, Leos embody a radiant energy that lights up any room, their magnanimous nature often making them the life of the party. They thrive on appreciation, love, and admiration, fueling their creative and passionate pursuits.

Leo's bold and vibrant essence finds a kindred spirit in the stimulating and uplifting effects of Sativa strains. These strains can enhance Leo's natural vivacity, fuel their creativity, and support their leadership qualities, ensuring they always find themselves in the limelight they so love and thrive in.

Recommended Strains for Leo

For Leos seeking to energize their spirit and inspire their heart's passions, the following Sativa strains are particularly fitting:

1. **Super Lemon Haze**: This zesty strain is perfect for the Leo looking to amplify their creative output and enjoy the spotlight. Super Lemon Haze offers a burst of energetic euphoria, sharpening focus and sparking joy, aligning well with Leo's sunny disposition.
2. **Strawberry Cough**: Known for its uplifting and euphoric effects, Strawberry Cough can enhance Leo's social prowess and charisma. Its ability to stimulate conversation and laughter makes it a great choice for social gatherings where Leo naturally shines.
3. **Durban Poison**: This pure Sativa is renowned for its energizing effects, which can fuel Leo's natural inclination towards leadership and action. Durban Poison is ideal for days when Leo seeks to conquer their goals with unmatched zeal.
4. **Tangie**: With its refreshing citrus flavor and uplifting effects, Tangie is another excellent choice for Leos. It encourages creativity,

joy, and an open heart, perfect for Leos engaging in artistic projects or simply living life with their trademark enthusiasm.

Cannabis Rituals for Leo

To further foster Leo's creativity, confidence, and joy, integrating the following cannabis rituals can enrich their royal journey:

1. **Creative Showcase**: Leos thrive when expressing themselves. Organize a gathering where you and your friends share your latest creative projects, from art to music to dance. Use a strain like Super Lemon Haze to stimulate creativity and ensure the spotlight shines brightly on each participant.

2. **Sunrise Salutations**: Embrace the energy of your ruling celestial body, the Sun, with a morning ritual. Consume a stimulating Sativa like Durban Poison before performing a series of Sun Salutations in yoga. This ritual can help align your inner energy with the sun's radiant power, invigorating your body and spirit for the day ahead.

3. **Joyful Journaling**: Set aside time to engage in joyful journaling, focusing on gratitude, aspirations, and positive affirmations. Accompany this practice with Tangie to elevate your mood and open your heart, allowing you to fully embrace and articulate your innermost desires and dreams.

4. **Social Spotlight Session**: Leos shine in social settings, and a session with Strawberry Cough can make social interactions even more delightful. Whether it's a party, a small gathering, or a virtual meet-up, this strain can enhance your natural charisma, making you the life of any gathering.

Through these recommended strains and rituals, "Celestial Cannabis: A Zodiac Journey" invites Leos to explore the energizing and uplifting world of Sativa strains. This journey is designed to magnify Leo's innate qualities of leadership, creativity, and love for the spotlight, ensuring they always remain the radiant and generous stars of their own lives.

If you want to see some amazing products, please visit my Virtual Dispensary: https://shift.store/sg1fan23477/retail

Chapter 6: Virgo – The Balanced Hybrid

Characteristics of Virgo

Virgo, represented by the Maiden, is the zodiac's epitome of precision, analytical prowess, and a diligent work ethic. Born between August 23rd and September 22nd, Virgos are known for their meticulous attention to detail, deep sense of humanity, and a constant pursuit of improvement and efficiency. Ruled by Mercury, the planet of communication, intellect, and reasoning, Virgos possess an impressive capacity to analyze and organize, making them the problem-solvers and healers of the zodiac. Despite their practical and sometimes critical outlook, Virgos have a deeply rooted desire to serve and improve, always aiming to refine themselves and their surroundings.

Virgo's analytical and meticulous nature finds harmony with the balanced effects of Hybrid strains. These strains, offering a mix of Sativa's cerebral clarity and Indica's calming relaxation, support Virgo's need for focus and productivity while providing a necessary counterbalance for relaxation and stress relief.

Recommended Strains for Virgo

For Virgos seeking to enhance their natural inclination towards organization, self-improvement, and meticulousness, the following Hybrid strains can offer the balanced support they need:

1. **Girl Scout Cookies (GSC):** This renowned Hybrid strain provides an excellent balance of physical relaxation with cerebral invigoration. GSC can help Virgos relax after a day of hard work, while still engaging the mind for creative problem-solving or planning.

2. **White Widow:** Offering a burst of euphoria and energy, followed by a state of deep relaxation, White Widow can stimulate Virgo's mind for high productivity phases, making it easier to tackle complex tasks that require a keen eye for detail.

3. **OG Kush:** Known for its stress-relieving properties, OG Kush can offer the mental clarity needed for Virgo's analytical tasks, while

also easing the physical tension that comes from prolonged periods of focus and dedication.

4. **Harlequin**: With a higher CBD content, Harlequin is ideal for Virgos who prefer a less intense psychoactive experience. It aids in maintaining focus and calm, perfect for methodical work, detailed analysis, or any activity requiring precision.

Cannabis Rituals for Virgo

Integrating cannabis into rituals that enhance organization, self-improvement, and health can significantly benefit Virgo's well-being and efficiency:

1. **Organized Mind Session**: Begin your day or a major project by consuming a strain like White Widow. Use the initial energy surge to organize your tasks, set goals, and plan your approach. As the relaxing effects set in, start tackling your tasks with precision and calm.

2. **Self-Improvement Study Breaks**: Virgos are naturally inclined towards self-improvement and learning. Pair study sessions or self-improvement activities with Harlequin to maintain focus without overwhelming stress. Take short breaks to consume and allow the CBD to enhance absorption and retention of new information.

3. **Health and Wellness Routine**: Incorporate OG Kush into your health and wellness routines, such as pre or post-workout sessions. The strain's balancing effects can enhance the physical activity's enjoyment and effectiveness, aligning with Virgo's focus on health and practical action.

4. **Mindful Decompression**: After a day of hard work and meticulous attention to detail, unwind with Girl Scout Cookies. Engage in a mindfulness or meditation practice to reflect on the day's achievements and areas for improvement, allowing the strain's effects to guide you towards relaxation and satisfaction.

Through these recommended strains and rituals, "Celestial Cannabis:

A Zodiac Journey" encourages Virgos to explore the harmonious balance offered by Hybrid strains. This exploration can support their innate qualities of meticulousness, organization, and a constant drive for improvement, providing a cannabis-fueled path to enhanced productivity, focus, and well-being.

If you want to see some amazing products, please visit my Virtual Dispensary: https://shift.store/sg1fan23477/retail

Chapter 7: Libra – The Harmony of Hybrids

Characteristics of Libra

Libra, represented by the Scales, is the zodiac sign that epitomizes balance, harmony, and a relentless pursuit of beauty and justice. Born between September 23rd and October 22nd, Librans are known for their diplomatic nature, social grace, and an eye for aesthetics that transcends the ordinary. Governed by Venus, the planet of love, art, and beauty, Librans are drawn to creating harmony in their surroundings and relationships, making peace and partnership their ultimate goals. Their air element endows them with excellent communication skills and an intellectual approach to solving problems, always seeking fairness and equilibrium in their interactions.

Libra's quest for balance and beauty finds a natural ally in the nuanced effects of Hybrid strains. These strains, with their balanced blend of Sativa's mental stimulation and Indica's physical relaxation, mirror Libra's own equilibrium, supporting their social nature and appreciation for the finer things in life.

Recommended Strains for Libra

For Librans seeking cannabis strains that reflect their inherent need for balance and enhance their appreciation for beauty and social connections, the following Hybrids are particularly well-suited:

1. **Blue Dream**: Offering a gentle cerebral invigoration followed by smooth physical relaxation, Blue Dream captures the essence of Libra's balance. It's perfect for social gatherings or enjoying the arts, as it enhances mood without overwhelming.

2. **Sour Diesel**: Known for its energizing effect that sparks creativity and conversation, Sour Diesel is ideal for Librans engaging in social debates or intellectual discussions. It fosters a sense of connection and elevates the discourse.

3. **Wedding Cake**: Rich in flavor and offering a balanced high,

Wedding Cake can enhance Libra's love for the sensory and the beautiful, making every experience more profound and satisfying, especially when shared with loved ones.

4. **Gelato**: For those artistic Librans seeking inspiration and a boost to their creative vision, Gelato provides a perfect blend of euphoria and relaxation, encouraging artistic expression and appreciation for beauty.

Cannabis Rituals for Libra

To enrich Libra's social interactions, artistic inclinations, and love for harmony, the following cannabis rituals can serve as a bridge to deeper connections and beauty appreciation:

1. **Artistic Collaboration Session**: Gather a group of friends for a creative jam session, be it painting, music, or any form of artistic expression. Use a strain like Gelato to stimulate creativity and open up new pathways of artistic communication, making the session a collaborative and harmonious experience.

2. **Social Justice Debate Night**: Libra's air element makes them natural debaters with a strong sense of justice. Organizing a debate night with friends, where Sour Diesel can stimulate thoughtful conversation and a respectful exchange of ideas, aligns perfectly with Libra's quest for balance and fairness.

3. **Cannabis-Infused Dinner Party**: Libra's love for social gatherings and fine food can be combined in a cannabis-infused dinner party. Blue Dream or Wedding Cake can enhance both the culinary experience and the social interaction, creating a harmonious atmosphere that celebrates Libra's love for beauty and companionship.

4. **Gallery Walk With a Twist**: Plan a visit to an art gallery or a scenic walk in a beautiful place, enhanced by consuming a strain like Blue Dream beforehand. This ritual can amplify Libra's natural appreciation for beauty and art, making each piece more vivid and each moment more profound.

Through these recommended strains and rituals, "Celestial Cannabis: A Zodiac Journey" invites Librans to explore the harmonious balance of Hybrid strains. This journey is tailored to enrich their social life, enhance their appreciation for art and beauty, and support their quest for balance, offering a path to deeper connections and more beautiful experiences.

If you want to see some amazing products, please visit my Virtual Dispensary: https://shift.store/sg1fan23477/retail

Chapter 8: Scorpio – Intense Indica Depths

Characteristics of Scorpio

Scorpio, symbolized by the Scorpion, is a sign that embodies intensity, passion, and a profound depth of emotions and mystery. Born between October 23rd and November 21st, Scorpios are known for their magnetic personalities, powerful presence, and a relentless desire to uncover the truth beneath the surface. Governed by Pluto, the planet of transformation and rebirth, Scorpios are naturally drawn to experiences that challenge them, leading to profound personal growth and change. Their water element bestows them with an intuitive and emotional depth that is unmatched, often making them excellent at understanding and navigating the unseen and the psychological.

Scorpio's intensity and transformative potential find a resonant echo in the deep, grounding effects of potent Indica strains. These strains offer a profound sense of relaxation and introspection, allowing Scorpios to delve into their inner worlds, explore their emotional depths, and undergo the transformation they seek.

Recommended Strains for Scorpio

For Scorpios seeking to match their depth with the transformative potential of cannabis, the following potent Indicas are particularly suitable:

1. **Purple Kush**: Known for its sedative effects and deep relaxation properties, Purple Kush can help Scorpios explore their inner depths in solitude or meditative practices, fostering profound introspective journeys.

2. **Bubba Kush**: Offering a tranquilizing effect that can help ease Scorpio's often tumultuous emotional waters, Bubba Kush is perfect for introspection and uncovering hidden truths within, encouraging emotional balance and peace.

3. **Blackwater**: Blackwater is a powerful Indica that can induce a deep state of relaxation and mental clarity, ideal for Scorpios looking to

meditate on their transformative journey and connect with their intuitive selves.

4. **Granddaddy Purple**: With its dreamy euphoria and physical relaxation, Granddaddy Purple is suited for Scorpios seeking to explore their psyche, enhance their spiritual practices, or simply unwind from their intense daily pursuits.

Cannabis Rituals for Scorpio

To support Scorpio's need for introspection, emotional exploration, and spiritual intimacy, the following cannabis rituals can serve as powerful tools for self-discovery and transformation:

1. **Deep Meditation Practice**: Incorporate a strain like Blackwater into your meditation practice, aiming to reach deeper states of consciousness and self-awareness. This ritual can help Scorpios uncover hidden aspects of themselves and facilitate profound personal growth.

2. **Journaling the Shadow Self**: Scorpios are naturally drawn to exploring their shadow self. Use Purple Kush to relax and enter a reflective state, then journal about your discoveries, fears, and dreams. This practice can lead to powerful insights and emotional healing.

3. **Spiritual Intimacy with a Partner**: Share a strain like Granddaddy Purple with a trusted partner to deepen your emotional and spiritual connection. Engage in honest, open conversations or practice tantra, focusing on deepening your bond and exploring the depths of intimacy together.

4. **Transformation Ritual**: On nights of the full moon, symbolic of transformation and renewal, consume Bubba Kush to facilitate a letting go of old patterns or beliefs. Perform a ritual that symbolizes this release, such as writing down what no longer serves you and burning the paper, allowing the transformative energy of Scorpio and the cannabis to guide you towards rebirth.

Through these recommended strains and practices, "Celestial Cannabis: A Zodiac Journey" invites Scorpios to dive deep into the intense Indica depths. This exploration not only aligns with their natural inclination towards transformation and introspection but also offers a pathway to profound emotional healing, spiritual intimacy, and self-discovery.

If you want to see some amazing products, please visit my Virtual Dispensary: https://shift.store/sg1fan23477/retail

Chapter 9: Sagittarius – Adventurous Sativa Horizons

Characteristics of Sagittarius

Sagittarius, symbolized by the Archer, is a sign characterized by its love for adventure, thirst for knowledge, and an ever-optimistic outlook on life. Born between November 22nd and December 21st, Sagittarians are known for their restless spirit, freedom-loving nature, and a philosophical mind that seeks to understand the deeper meanings of life. Ruled by Jupiter, the planet of growth, expansion, and fortune, Sagittarians are drawn to experiences that expand their horizons, whether through physical travel, intellectual pursuits, or exploring the realms of spirituality and belief systems. Their fire element fuels their passion for life and desire for constant exploration and adventure.

Sagittarius' adventurous and expansive spirit finds a perfect match in the uplifting and energizing effects of Sativa strains. These strains inspire exploration, enhance creativity, and foster expansive thinking, aligning with Sagittarius' quest for knowledge and new experiences.

Recommended Strains for Sagittarius

For Sagittarians seeking to complement their adventurous spirit and love for learning, the following uplifting Sativas are ideally suited:

1. **Super Silver Haze**: Known for its energetic and uplifting high, Super Silver Haze can inspire Sagittarians to embark on new adventures or tackle philosophical inquiries with renewed vigor and clarity.

2. **Green Crack**: This strain offers a sharp, energizing effect that can fuel a Sagittarian's long quests for exploration and understanding, keeping them motivated and focused on their journey.

3. **Jack Herer**: Named after the famed cannabis activist, Jack Herer stimulates creativity and provides a blissful, clear-headed experience, ideal for Sagittarians engaging in creative problem-solving or exploring new ideas.

4. **Amnesia Haze**: With its cerebral high and mood-lifting effects, Amnesia Haze is perfect for those moments when Sagittarius seeks to expand their mind, whether through studying, meditation, or philosophical discussions.

Cannabis Rituals for Sagittarius

To align with Sagittarius' love for adventure, learning, and spiritual exploration, the following cannabis rituals can enhance their experiences:

1. **Travel Companion Ritual**: Before setting off on a new adventure, consume a strain like Super Silver Haze to heighten your senses and awareness of the beauty and novelty around you. Let cannabis be your companion as you explore new landscapes, cultures, and ideas.

2. **Philosophical Discussion Nights**: Organize gatherings with friends where you discuss philosophical, spiritual, or metaphysical topics. Use Jack Herer to stimulate thought-provoking conversations and open your minds to different perspectives.

3. **Creative Exploration Sessions**: Engage in creative pursuits such as painting, writing, or music with the help of Green Crack. Allow the strain to enhance your creativity and inspire innovative ideas, fueling your artistic expressions with a spirit of adventure.

4. **Spiritual Quests**: For those moments of introspection and spiritual seeking, Amnesia Haze can offer the mood-lifting and mind-expanding effects needed to deepen your meditation practices or explore various spiritual teachings and practices.

Through these recommended strains and rituals, "Celestial Cannabis: A Zodiac Journey" invites Sagittarians to embrace the adventurous Sativa horizons. This journey is designed to complement their natural inclination towards exploration, growth, and the pursuit of knowledge, providing a pathway to enriching experiences and expansive thinking.

If you want to see some amazing products, please visit my Virtual Dispensary: https://shift.store/sg1fan23477/retail

Chapter 10: Capricorn – The Indica Achievement

Characteristics of Capricorn

Capricorn, represented by the Sea-Goat, is the zodiac sign that embodies discipline, ambition, and a steadfast approach to life's challenges and opportunities. Born between December 22nd and January 19th, Capricorns are known for their pragmatic, goal-oriented nature, and an unwavering focus on their aspirations. Ruled by Saturn, the planet of responsibility and structure, Capricorns possess a remarkable resilience and a deep sense of duty that drives them to achieve and excel in their endeavors. Their earth element grounds them, providing a stable foundation upon which they methodically build their successes, often embodying the epitome of self-control and leadership.

Capricorn's disciplined and ambitious nature finds solace and support in the grounding and focusing effects of Indica strains. These strains offer relaxation and mental clarity, allowing Capricorns to recharge after periods of intense effort and to maintain their focus on long-term goals without succumbing to burnout.

Recommended Strains for Capricorn

For Capricorns seeking to complement their hardworking ethos and need for restorative rest, the following grounding Indicas are especially suitable:

1. **Northern Lights**: Famed for its ability to induce deep relaxation and relieve stress, Northern Lights can help Capricorns unwind after a day of relentless pursuit of their goals, aiding in recovery and preparation for future challenges.
2. **Afghan Kush**: Originating from the Hindu Kush mountain range, this pure Indica is ideal for promoting a sense of calm and mental clarity, perfect for Capricorns needing to decompress and reflect on their achievements.
3. **Blueberry**: Known for its relaxing effects and ability to induce a state of happy euphoria, Blueberry can provide Capricorns with

the mental break needed to enjoy the fruits of their labor, encouraging moments of leisure and contentment.

4. **Granddaddy Purple**: Offering both physical relaxation and a dreamy mental state, Granddaddy Purple is suited for Capricorns seeking to balance their disciplined nature with necessary periods of dreaming and visualization, essential for setting new goals and aspirations.

Cannabis Rituals for Capricorn

To align with Capricorn's disciplined approach to goal-setting, perseverance, and the need for restorative rest, the following cannabis rituals can enhance their journey towards achievement:

1. **Goal Visualization Session**: Before starting a new project or phase of work, Capricorns can engage in a goal visualization session with a strain like Granddaddy Purple. This ritual involves meditating on one's aspirations, using the strain's dreamy effects to visualize success and the steps needed to achieve it.

2. **Perseverance Practice**: In moments of doubt or when faced with obstacles, consuming Afghan Kush can offer the calm and clarity needed to navigate challenges. Use this time to reassess strategies and reaffirm commitment to your goals, reinforcing your path with renewed determination.

3. **Restorative Rest Ritual**: After achieving a milestone, Capricorns should prioritize restorative rest to recharge their mental and physical energy. A session with Northern Lights before bedtime can ensure deep, restful sleep, allowing for recovery and rejuvenation.

4. **Leisure and Enjoyment Break**: It's essential for Capricorns to remember to enjoy the journey towards their goals. Scheduling regular leisure breaks with a strain like Blueberry can provide necessary moments of relaxation and happiness, reminding them to appreciate the present and the beauty of their efforts.

Through these recommended strains and practices, "Celestial

Cannabis: A Zodiac Journey" invites Capricorns to embrace the grounding and focusing qualities of Indica strains. This exploration supports their disciplined and ambitious nature, offering pathways to achieving their goals while ensuring they remain grounded and replenished on their journey to the pinnacle of success.

If you want to see some amazing products, please visit my Virtual Dispensary: https://shift.store/sg1fan23477/retail

Chapter 11: Aquarius – The Sativa Innovation

Characteristics of Aquarius

Aquarius, symbolized by the Water Bearer, is a zodiac sign known for its innovative spirit, eccentricity, and strong humanitarian instincts. Born between January 20th and February 18th, Aquarians are forward-thinking visionaries who cherish independence, freedom, and the pursuit of novel ideas. Ruled by Uranus, the planet of breakthroughs, revolution, and unexpected changes, Aquarians thrive on the edge of societal norms, always seeking to challenge the status quo and bring about progressive changes. Their air element endows them with a high intellect and a penchant for conceptual thinking, making them excellent problem solvers and pioneers of new movements.

Aquarius' innovative and eccentric traits resonate well with the stimulating and mind-expanding effects of Sativa strains. These strains encourage creativity, enhance social awareness, and promote unconventional thinking, aligning with Aquarius' quest for innovation and social reform.

Recommended Strains for Aquarius

For Aquarians seeking to enhance their visionary qualities and support their humanitarian endeavors, the following stimulating Sativas are ideally suited:

1. **Sour Diesel**: Known for its energizing and cerebral effects, Sour Diesel can ignite Aquarius' innovative thinking and fuel their drive for social change, enhancing their ability to brainstorm groundbreaking ideas.

2. **Super Silver Haze**: Offering a euphoric and uplifting experience, Super Silver Haze can stimulate creativity and inspire Aquarius to connect with their visionary ideas, making it easier to conceptualize new inventions or artistic projects.

3. **Green Crack**: This strain provides a sharp, focused energy that can help Aquarians maintain their momentum on long-term projects or activism campaigns, keeping them engaged and motivated.

4. **Amnesia Haze**: With its mood-lifting and mind-expanding effects, Amnesia Haze is perfect for deep philosophical discussions or exploring new perspectives, ideal for the intellectually curious Aquarius.

Cannabis Rituals for Aquarius

To align with Aquarius' passion for community building, activism, and creative expression, the following cannabis rituals can foster their innovative spirit and commitment to making a difference:

1. **Community Brainstorming Sessions**: Organize group sessions with like-minded individuals to tackle social issues, using Sour Diesel to energize the group and enhance creative problem-solving. This ritual fosters a sense of community and collective action towards common goals.

2. **Artistic Innovation Workshops**: Engage in workshops or solo sessions focused on creating art that challenges conventional norms, with the help of Super Silver Haze to inspire unconventional creativity. These practices can serve as a medium for Aquarius to express their visionary ideas and insights.

3. **Activism Planning Gatherings**: Use Green Crack during planning sessions for activism campaigns or community projects, allowing its focused energy to aid in organizing effective strategies and actions that reflect Aquarius' humanitarian values.

4. **Philosophical Exploration Nights**: Facilitate gatherings or solo sessions dedicated to exploring philosophical theories, futuristic concepts, or new technologies, enhanced by Amnesia Haze's mind-expanding properties. This ritual encourages deep thought, reflection, and discussion, aligning with Aquarius' love for intellectual exploration.

Through these recommended strains and rituals, "Celestial Cannabis: A Zodiac Journey" invites Aquarians to explore the stimulating world of Sativa strains. This journey is designed to complement their innovative spirit, fostering creativity, social awareness, and the pursuit of unconventional ideas, thereby supporting their endeavors to bring about positive change and progress in the world.

If you want to see some amazing products, please visit my Virtual Dispensary: https://shift.store/sg1fan23477/retail

Chapter 12: Pisces – The Ethereal Indica

Characteristics of Pisces

Pisces, symbolized by the Two Fish swimming in opposite directions, is the zodiac sign that embodies the essence of dreaminess, compassion, and profound spiritual depth. Born between February 19th and March 20th, Pisceans are recognized for their empathetic nature, artistic inclinations, and an intrinsic connection to the mystical aspects of life. Ruled by Neptune, the planet of dreams, intuition, and illusion, Pisceans often find themselves floating between reality and the ethereal realms, seeking to merge the tangible with the transcendent. Their water element enhances their emotional sensitivity and predisposes them to absorb the feelings and energies of their environment, further deepening their compassionate and understanding nature.

Pisces' dreamy and spiritual essence finds solace and amplification in the calming and introspective effects of Indica strains and CBD-rich cannabis. These varieties can facilitate emotional depth, enhance meditative states, and support Pisces in their exploration of the spiritual and the imaginative.

Recommended Strains for Pisces

For Pisceans seeking to deepen their emotional and spiritual explorations, the following dreamy Indicas and CBD strains are particularly suitable:

1. **Granddaddy Purple**: Offering deep physical relaxation and a cerebral dreaminess, Granddaddy Purple is ideal for Pisces looking to explore their subconscious and enhance their meditative practices.

2. **Blue Dream**: While predominantly Sativa, Blue Dream's calming Indica effects make it perfect for Pisces' artistic endeavors, providing the relaxation needed for creative flow while stimulating the mind.

3. **ACDC**: A high-CBD strain known for its minimal psychoactive effects, ACDC can help Pisces maintain emotional balance while

exploring spiritual practices or when seeking solace from the over-whelm of their empathetic nature.

4. **Northern Lights**: This pure Indica strain induces deep relaxation and mental ease, allowing Pisces to connect more profoundly with their inner selves and the universal consciousness, facilitating spiritual insights and peaceful introspection.

Cannabis Rituals for Pisces

To nurture Pisces' connection with the spiritual, artistic, and their compassionate essence, the following cannabis rituals can serve as gateways to deeper understanding and expression:

1. **Meditative Immersion**: Begin or end your day with a meditative session accompanied by Granddaddy Purple, focusing on deep breathing and visualization to connect with the universal energy. This practice can help Pisces dissolve boundaries, fostering a sense of oneness and spiritual clarity.

2. **Creative Flow Sessions**: Use Blue Dream as a catalyst for artistic expression, whether through painting, writing, music, or any other form of art. Allow the strain to guide your intuition and creativity, making your artistic practice a spiritual journey of self-discovery.

3. **Empathetic Healing Rituals**: For moments of emotional overwhelm, ACDC can provide the grounding and centering needed for Pisces to process and release absorbed energies. Engage in self-care rituals that reinforce boundaries and cleanse your emotional palette, such as salt baths, journaling, or yoga.

4. **Cosmic Connection Practices**: Under the night sky, consume Northern Lights to deepen your connection with the cosmos. Contemplate the stars, the moon, and the vastness of the universe, allowing the experience to enhance your spiritual perspective and remind you of the interconnectedness of all things.

Through these recommended strains and practices, "Celestial Cannabis: A Zodiac Journey" invites Pisceans to embrace the ethereal qualities of Indica and CBD-rich strains. This exploration supports their spiritual journey, artistic expression, and emotional depth, offering pathways to profound introspection, creative inspiration, and a harmonious connection with the universal consciousness.

If you want to see some amazing products, please visit my Virtual Dispensary: https://shift.store/sg1fan23477/retail

Conclusion: The Celestial Cannabis Constellation

As we conclude our journey through the zodiac, weaving together the threads of celestial wisdom with the grounding roots of cannabis, we find ourselves within a vast constellation of experiences and insights. "Celestial Cannabis: A Zodiac Journey" has been an exploration not just of the individual characteristics that align each sign with specific cannabis strains and rituals, but of a deeper, holistic understanding of how cannabis can be a tool for personal growth, healing, and self-discovery.

Integrating the Journey

Each sign's journey through the realms of cannabis has revealed unique pathways to balance, creativity, introspection, and spiritual awakening. From the fiery ambition of Aries guided by energizing Sativas to the dreamy depths of Pisces soothed by ethereal Indicas, we've seen how cannabis can act as a mirror reflecting our innermost selves and as a key unlocking doors to new realms of understanding. This journey emphasizes the diversity of cannabis experiences and the personalized ways in which it can enhance our lives, echoing the vast array of human expressions found within the zodiac.

Personalized Pathways

As you reflect on this journey, consider your sun sign's natural affinities with certain cannabis strains and rituals but don't stop there. Explore how your moon sign influences your emotional inner world and how your rising sign affects your outward expression and experiences. Delve into the alignments and aspects of your full astrological chart to discover a multifaceted approach to your cannabis journey. This exploration is a deeply personal one, where intuition and introspection lead the way to discovering how cannabis can best support your individual path. Let your experiences, guided by the stars, be your teacher as you learn to navigate this journey in a way that resonates with your true self.

The Cosmic Connection Continued

This book is but an invitation to a lifelong exploration of the nexus between the celestial and the cannabis journey. The cosmic connection, woven through the tapestry of our lives, offers endless opportunities for growth, healing, and transformation. As the planets continue their eternal dance through the cosmos, so too does our understanding of ourselves deepen with each experience. Cannabis, with its rich tapestry of strains and effects, offers a unique lens through which to view our lives, challenges, and aspirations.

As you continue on your celestial cannabis journey, remember that the stars offer guidance, not determinism. The power to shape your path lies within you, with cannabis serving as a companion and tool for exploration. Embrace the journey with an open heart and mind, allowing the cosmic wisdom to illuminate your path and cannabis to ground your experiences in the physical realm.

"Celestial Cannabis: A Zodiac Journey" is your invitation to explore, to dream, and to connect more deeply with both the universe around you and the universe within. May this journey be one of discovery, transformation, and profound connection, as you navigate the celestial cannabis constellation with curiosity, courage, and an open heart.

Appendix A: Cannabis Glossary

This glossary serves as a comprehensive guide to the terminology associated with cannabis culture, science, and law. It is designed to demystify the complex language surrounding cannabis, making the world of cannabis more accessible to enthusiasts, patients, researchers, and the general public.

A

- **Anandamide**: An endocannabinoid produced naturally in the body that binds to cannabinoid receptors, influencing bodily functions such as appetite, memory, and pain.
- **Autoflowering**: A type of cannabis plant that automatically transitions from the vegetative stage to the flowering stage with age, rather than in response to light cycle changes.

B

- **BHO (Butane Hash Oil)**: A potent concentrate of cannabinoids made by dissolving cannabis in butane. Known for its high THC content.
- **Bud**: The flower of the cannabis plant, harvested for medicinal or recreational use due to its concentration of cannabinoids and terpenes.

C

- **CBD (Cannabidiol)**: A non-psychoactive cannabinoid known for its potential therapeutic effects, including reducing inflammation and anxiety.
- **CBG (Cannabigerol)**: A non-psychoactive cannabinoid, often referred to as the "mother of all cannabinoids," because other cannabinoids are derived from its acid form, CBGA.
- **Cannabinoids**: Chemical compounds found in cannabis that interact with the body's endocannabinoid system to produce various effects.
- **Cannabis**: A genus of flowering plants in the family Cannabaceae, which includes species commonly known as marijuana and hemp.
- **Concentrates**: Highly potent substances made by extracting cannabinoids and terpenes from the cannabis plant. Examples include hash, wax, and oils.

D

- **Decarboxylation**: A process that activates cannabinoids in cannabis through heat, making them available for absorption by the body.
- **Dabbing**: A method of consuming cannabis concentrates by vaporizing them on a hot surface and inhaling the vapor.

E

- **Edibles**: Food products infused with cannabis extracts, consumed for medicinal or recreational effects.
- **Endocannabinoid System (ECS)**: A complex cell-signaling system identified in the 1990s that plays a role in regulating a range of functions and processes, including sleep, mood, appetite, and memory.

F

- **Feminized Seeds**: Cannabis seeds that have been bred to produce female plants exclusively, ensuring that all plants will produce buds.

H

- **Hemp**: A variety of Cannabis sativa plant species grown primarily for the industrial uses of its derived products. It is low in THC and can be used to make a variety of products including textiles, biofuel, and health foods.

I

- **Indica**: A species or variety of cannabis known for producing a body high, typically used for its relaxing and sedative effects.

M

- **Microdosing**: The practice of consuming small, sub-psychoactive doses of cannabis to achieve the desired medical benefits without experiencing a significant alteration in mood or perception.

P

- **Phenotype**: The set of observable characteristics of a cannabis plant resulting from the interaction of its genetic makeup with the environment.
- **Psychoactive**: Substances that change brain function and result in alterations in perception, mood, consciousness, cognition, or behavior.

R

- **Rosin**: A solventless cannabis concentrate made by applying heat and pressure to cannabis flowers or kief, resulting in the extraction of the resin.

S

- **Sativa**: A species or variety of cannabis known for producing a cerebral, energizing high, often used for its uplifting effects.
- **Strain**: A specific variety of cannabis plant, bred for certain characteristics like flavor, aroma, effect, and yield.
- **Synthetic Cannabinoids**: Man-made chemicals designed to mimic the effects of natural cannabinoids, often with much stronger and unpredictable effects.

T

- **Terpenes**: Aromatic compounds found in many plants, including cannabis, responsible for the plant's fragrance and flavor. Terpenes may also influence the effects of cannabis by modulating the activity of cannabinoids.
- **THC (Tetrahydrocannabinol)**: The main psychoactive compound in cannabis, responsible for the high sensation.
- **Tincture**: A cannabis-infused liquid solution, often alcohol-based, consumed orally or sublingually (under the tongue).

V

- **Vaporizer**: A device used to consume cannabis by heating the flower or concentrate to a temperature that vaporizes, but does not burn, the cannabinoids and terpenes, producing a vapor to be inhaled.

This glossary is intended as a starting point for those seeking to deepen their understanding of cannabis and its multifaceted role in culture, science, and law. As the cannabis landscape continues to evolve, so too will the language we use to describe and navigate it.

Appendix B: Cannabis Strain Directory

This directory serves as a comprehensive guide to some of the most notable cannabis strains across the Sativa, Indica, and hybrid categories. Each entry highlights the strain's origins, typical effects, and potential medicinal uses, offering a window into the rich diversity within the cannabis species. This resource is designed for educational purposes, to assist enthusiasts, patients, and the curious in navigating the vast universe of cannabis strains.

<u>**Sativa Strains**</u>

1. Sour Diesel

- **Origins**: Believed to have descended from Chemdawg 91 and Super Skunk.
- **Typical Effects**: Energizing, dreamy cerebral effects that have pushed Sour Diesel to its legendary status. Expect a fast-acting invigorating high.
- **Medicinal Uses**: Often used to alleviate depression, pain, and fatigue.

2. Green Crack

- **Origins**: Mythically linked to Snoop Dogg, this strain boasts an energetic and uplifting high. Its lineage is often disputed, though it's generally believed to be a cross between Skunk #1 and an unknown Indica.
- **Typical Effects**: Sharp energy and focus as it induces an invigorating mental buzz.
- **Medicinal Uses**: Ideal for treating fatigue, stress, and depression.

3. Jack Herer

- **Origins**: A tribute to the famed cannabis activist, this strain is a cross between Haze, Northern Lights #5, and Shiva Skunk.
- **Typical Effects**: A blissful, clear-headed, and creative high.
- **Medicinal Uses**: Used for treating low energy, depression, and fatigue.

Indica Strains

1. Northern Lights

- **Origins**: One of the most famous Indicas, its lineage is thought to have originated from indigenous Afghani and Thai landrace strains.
- **Typical Effects**: Comforting euphoria followed by relaxation.
- **Medicinal Uses**: Highly effective for pain relief, stress, and insomnia.

2. Granddaddy Purple

- **Origins**: Created by Ken Estes in 2003, this strain is a well-known Indica cross between Purple Urkle and Big Bud.
- **Typical Effects**: Famous for its dreamy euphoria that blankets the mind in calmness.
- **Medicinal Uses**: Ideal for pain, stress, insomnia, appetite loss, and muscle spasms.

3. Afghan Kush

- **Origins**: Stemming from the Hindu Kush mountain range near the Afghanistan-Pakistan border.
- **Typical Effects**: Deep relaxation and euphoria, presenting a heavy body sensation.
- **Medicinal Uses**: Often sought for its heavy resin content and powerfully sedating effects, useful in treating insomnia, pain, and stress disorders.

Hybrid Strains

1. Blue Dream

- **Origins**: A sativa-dominant hybrid originating in California, has achieved legendary West Coast status. It's a cross between Blueberry indica and sativa Haze.
- **Typical Effects**: Balances full-body relaxation with a gentle cerebral invigoration.
- **Medicinal Uses**: Popular for daytime treatment of symptoms of depression, chronic pain, and nausea.

2. GG4 (Gorilla Glue #4)

- **Origins**: A potent hybrid strain that delivers heavy-handed euphoria and relaxation, leaving you feeling "glued" to the couch. Its origins trace back to Chem's Sister, Sour Dubb, and Chocolate Diesel.
- **Typical Effects**: Heavy sedation and euphoria.
- **Medicinal Uses**: Used for treating pain, stress, and depression.

3. GSC (Girl Scout Cookies)

- **Origins**: An OG Kush and Durban Poison hybrid cross whose reputation grew too large to stay within the borders of its California homeland.
- **Typical Effects**: Offers a euphoric high and strong feelings of relaxation.
- **Medicinal Uses**: Effective at treating anxiety, stress, and depression, appetite loss, and chronic pain.

This directory is not exhaustive but represents a curated selection of strains known for their distinctive effects and medicinal properties. The cannabis landscape is constantly evolving, with new strains and genetics emerging as breeders mix and match genetics to achieve new heights in flavor, potency, and therapeutic efficacy. As you explore these strains, remember that the effects of cannabis can vary widely among individuals, influenced by factors such as tolerance, consumption method, and the plant's cannabinoid and terpene profiles.

Appendix C: Legal Status by Region

The legal status of cannabis varies dramatically around the world, reflecting a complex patchwork of laws and regulations that govern its use, cultivation, possession, and sale. This appendix provides an overview of cannabis legality in various countries and states, highlighting the distinctions between medicinal and recreational use. It's important to note that laws are continually evolving, and while this appendix offers a snapshot of current regulations, always verify the latest legal status in your area.

North America
United States

- **Medicinal Use:** Legal in 33 states, plus the District of Columbia, Guam, Puerto Rico, and the U.S. Virgin Islands.
- **Recreational Use:** Legal in 11 states and the District of Columbia. Note that cannabis remains illegal at the federal level.

Canada

- **Medicinal Use:** Legal nationwide since 2001.
- **Recreational Use:** Legal nationwide since October 17, 2018.

Mexico

- **Medicinal Use:** Legal with restrictions since June 2017.
- **Recreational Use:** Supreme Court decriminalized personal use in a landmark ruling, but comprehensive legislation is pending.

Europe
Netherlands

- **Medicinal Use:** Legal.
- **Recreational Use:** Decriminalized; sale and consumption allowed in licensed coffee shops.

Germany

- **Medicinal Use:** Legal since March 2017.
- **Recreational Use:** Possession of small amounts decriminalized; full legalization discussions are ongoing.

Portugal

- **Medicinal Use:** Legal since 2018.
- **Recreational Use:** Decriminalized since 2001 for personal use.

Oceania
Australia

- **Medicinal Use:** Legal nationwide since February 2016.
- **Recreational Use:** Illegal at the federal level; however, the Australian Capital Territory legalized possession and growth for personal use in January 2020.

New Zealand

- **Medicinal Use:** Legal with prescription since April 2020.
- **Recreational Use:** Illegal, though a referendum in October 2020 narrowly failed to legalize.

Asia
Thailand

- **Medicinal Use:** Legalized in December 2018.

- **Recreational Use:** Illegal, with harsh penalties for possession and trafficking.

India

- **Medicinal Use:** Legal in certain states.
- **Recreational Use:** Illegal at the national level, though enforcement varies by state. Traditional use in certain religious contexts.

South America
Uruguay

- **Medicinal Use:** Legal.
- **Recreational Use:** First country in the world to fully legalize the sale, cultivation, and consumption of cannabis in December 2013.

Colombia

- **Medicinal Use:** Legal.
- **Recreational Use:** Decriminalized for personal use. Legal framework for medical cannabis is well-established.

Africa
South Africa

- **Medicinal Use:** Legal with a prescription.
- **Recreational Use:** The Constitutional Court decriminalized the private use and cultivation in September 2018.

This overview illustrates the varied approaches to cannabis legislation worldwide, ranging from full prohibition to complete legalization. The trend towards legalization, especially for medicinal purposes, reflects a growing recognition of cannabis's therapeutic benefits. However, the landscape is complex and rapidly changing, underscoring the importance of staying informed about the laws in your specific region. Always consult local regulations and legal advice when navigating the legalities of cannabis use, cultivation, or possession.

Appendix D: Cultivation Tips

Cultivating cannabis can be a rewarding experience, offering insights into the plant's lifecycle and the satisfaction of harvesting your own buds. Whether you're a novice gardener or a seasoned grower, understanding the basics of cannabis cultivation is crucial for success. This appendix covers essential cultivation tips for both indoor and outdoor setups, including strain selection, light cycles, nutrient requirements, pest management, and harvesting techniques.

Choosing the Right Strain

- **Research**: Begin by researching strains that are well-suited to your growing environment and meet your needs in terms of effects, flavor, and medicinal properties.
- **Climate Compatibility**: For outdoor grows, choose strains that will thrive in your climate. Sativas generally prefer warmer climates, while Indicas are better suited for cooler conditions.
- **Space Considerations**: Indica strains tend to be bushier and shorter, making them ideal for indoor grows with limited space. Sativas, on the other hand, can grow tall and are more suited to outdoor gardens.

Understanding the Light Cycle

- **Vegetative Stage**: Cannabis plants require long periods of light (about 18 hours) and 6 hours of darkness to stay in the vegetative stage, where they develop their size and structure.
- **Flowering Stage**: To initiate flowering, plants need longer periods of darkness (12 hours of light/12 hours of darkness). This mimics the changing seasons and tells the plant it's time to produce flowers.

- **Light Quality**: Use full-spectrum lights for indoor grows to mimic natural sunlight. LED lights are energy-efficient and produce less heat, making them a popular choice among indoor cultivators.

Nutrient Requirements

- **Growth Stages**: Cannabis plants have different nutrient needs during the vegetative and flowering stages. Use a nitrogen-rich fertilizer during vegetative growth and switch to a phosphorus and potassium-rich fertilizer during flowering.
- **pH Levels**: Maintain the soil or hydroponic solution at a pH level between 6.0 and 7.0 to ensure that plants can absorb nutrients effectively.
- **Overfeeding**: Be cautious of overfeeding, which can lead to nutrient burn and damage your plants. Follow nutrient guidelines and observe plant responses to adjust as necessary.

Pest Management

- **Prevention**: The best strategy is prevention. Keep your grow area clean, and monitor your plants regularly for signs of pests or disease.
- **Natural Solutions**: Use natural pest control methods, such as introducing beneficial insects, using neem oil, or applying diatomaceous earth to soil to manage pests without resorting to harmful chemicals.
- **Quarantine**: Immediately isolate any plants that show signs of pest infestation or disease to prevent spread to healthy plants.

Harvesting Techniques

- **Timing**: Harvest time is critical for maximizing potency and flavor. Indicators of readiness include the darkening of pistils and the cloudiness of trichomes when viewed under a magnifying glass.

- **Drying and Curing**: After harvesting, dry your buds slowly in a dark, ventilated space. Once dry, cure the buds in airtight jars, opening them daily for the first week to release moisture and allow for even curing.
- **Patience**: The drying and curing process can take several weeks but is crucial for enhancing the flavor, potency, and smoothness of your cannabis.

Cultivating cannabis requires attention to detail, patience, and a willingness to learn from each grow cycle. By understanding the basics outlined in this guide and continuously seeking out new information and techniques, you can optimize your cultivation practices and enjoy the fruits of your labor. Remember, the key to successful cannabis cultivation is not just in the science but in the art of nurturing your plants through each stage of their growth.

Appendix E: Consumption Methods

Cannabis offers a versatile range of consumption methods, each with unique benefits, onset times, and durations of effects. Understanding these methods can help users choose the best option for their needs, whether for medicinal purposes or recreational enjoyment. This appendix explores the primary ways to consume cannabis, including smoking, vaporization, edibles, tinctures, and topicals.

Smoking

- **Methods**: Includes joints, blunts, pipes, and bongs.
- **Onset Time**: Effects are almost immediate, typically felt within minutes.
- **Duration**: Effects can last between 1 to 3 hours, varying by individual tolerance and the amount consumed.
- **Considerations**: Smoking is the most traditional method but poses health risks due to inhalation of combustion byproducts. It's effective for those seeking quick relief or immediate effects.

Vaporization

- **Methods**: Utilizes dry herb vaporizers or vape pens with cannabis concentrates.
- **Onset Time**: Effects are rapid, similar to smoking, felt within minutes.
- **Duration**: Effects generally last 1 to 3 hours, depending on the dosage and individual.
- **Considerations**: Vaporization is considered a healthier alternative to smoking, as it heats cannabis to a point where cannabinoids are released without burning the plant material, reducing inhalation of harmful substances.

Edibles

- **Methods**: Cannabis-infused foods and drinks.
- **Onset Time**: Onset is delayed, typically felt within 30 minutes to 2 hours after consumption.
- **Duration**: Effects are longer-lasting, ranging from 4 to 8 hours, sometimes extending up to 12 hours.
- **Considerations**: The delayed onset and prolonged effects of edibles make dosage control crucial. Start with a low dose and wait to understand the full effects before consuming more.

Tinctures

- **Methods**: Cannabis extracts dissolved in alcohol or oil, administered sublingually (under the tongue).
- **Onset Time**: Effects can begin within 15 to 30 minutes when taken sublingually; if swallowed, effects are similar to edibles.
- **Duration**: Effects can last between 4 to 6 hours.
- **Considerations**: Tinctures offer a discreet and dose-controlled way to consume cannabis. They're particularly suitable for medicinal users seeking the therapeutic benefits without inhalation.

Topicals

- **Methods**: Cannabis-infused lotions, balms, and oils applied directly to the skin.
- **Onset Time**: Varies widely based on the product's formulation but generally takes effect within minutes of application.
- **Duration**: Can last several hours, depending on the product's potency and the issue being addressed.
- **Considerations**: Topicals are ideal for localized relief of pain, inflammation, or skin conditions. They do not typically produce psychoactive effects, making them appealing for those seeking therapeutic benefits without the "high."

Additional Methods
Concentrates

- **Methods**: Includes wax, shatter, and oil, consumed through dabbing or with special vaporizers.
- **Onset Time**: Effects are almost immediate.
- **Duration**: Depending on the potency, effects can last 1 to 3 hours.
- **Considerations**: Concentrates are highly potent and recommended for experienced users. They offer intense effects and flavors but require special equipment.

Capsules

- **Methods**: Cannabis oil or powder encapsulated for oral consumption.
- **Onset Time**: Similar to edibles, usually 30 minutes to 2 hours.
- **Duration**: Effects can last 4 to 8 hours.
- **Considerations**: Capsules provide a discreet, dose-controlled way to consume cannabis, ideal for medicinal users who need consistent dosing without inhalation or taste.

Choosing the right consumption method depends on individual needs, preferences, and the desired effects. For medicinal users, considerations of onset time and duration of effects are particularly important for symptom management. Recreational users may choose based on convenience, preference for the experience, or health considerations. Regardless of the method, starting with a low dose and going slow is key to finding the optimal experience.

Appendix F: Recommended Reading and Resources

For enthusiasts, patients, cultivators, and researchers alike, a wealth of knowledge on cannabis awaits exploration. This curated list of books, scientific articles, websites, and forums offers a comprehensive guide to deepen your understanding of cannabis. From historical texts to contemporary scientific research, and from cultivation techniques to cultural studies, these resources provide valuable insights into the multifaceted world of cannabis.

Books

1. "The Emperor Wears No Clothes" by Jack Herer

- A classic in cannabis literature, this book details the history of cannabis prohibition and its uses as a renewable source of medicine, energy, food, and fiber.

2. "Cannabis Pharmacy: The Practical Guide to Medical Marijuana" by Michael Backes

- Offers an in-depth exploration of the medical applications of cannabis, detailing the science of how cannabinoids work and how to use cannabis for various conditions.

3. "Marijuana Horticulture: The Indoor/Outdoor Medical Grower's Bible" by Jorge Cervantes

- A comprehensive guide to cultivating high-quality cannabis, covering everything from seed selection to harvesting, for both indoor and outdoor growers.

4. "The Cannabis Manifesto: A New Paradigm for Wellness" by Steve DeAngelo

- This book delves into the health and wellness potential of cannabis, arguing for the end of prohibition and the embrace of cannabis as a tool for healing.

5. "Cannabis and CBD for Health and Wellness" by Aliza Sherman and Dr. Junella Chin

- An introductory guide to the therapeutic uses of cannabis and CBD, including how to select and administer CBD for various health benefits.

Scientific Articles

1. "The Endocannabinoid System and its Therapeutic Exploitation" in Nature Reviews Drug Discovery

- Provides a thorough overview of the endocannabinoid system and its potential targets for drug development.

2. "Taming THC: Potential Cannabis Synergy and Phytocannabinoid-Terpenoid Entourage Effects" in the British Journal of Pharmacology

- Explores the synergistic effects of cannabinoids and terpenes, contributing to the "entourage effect" and potential therapeutic applications.

3. "Cannabidiol: Pharmacology and Potential Therapeutic Role in Epilepsy and Other Neuropsychiatric Disorders" in Epilepsia

- Reviews the pharmacology of CBD and its potential in treating epilepsy and other neuropsychiatric disorders.

Websites

1. Leafly (leafly.com)

- A comprehensive resource for strain reviews, dispensary locations, and cannabis news.

2. Project CBD (projectcbd.org)

- Focuses on CBD research and education, offering resources on CBD's medical benefits and how to use it effectively.

3. NORML (norml.org)

- Advocacy organization with resources on cannabis laws, medical information, and activism.

Forums and Online Communities

1. r/microgrowery and r/cannabiscultivation on Reddit

- Subreddits focused on cannabis cultivation, offering advice, troubleshooting, and community support.

2. Grasscity Forums (forums.grasscity.com)

- One of the oldest online cannabis community forums, covering a wide range of topics from cultivation to consumption and legal issues.

3. ICMag (icmag.com)

- International Cannagraphic Magazine Forums offer a platform for growers to share techniques, grow journals, and cannabis photography.

This list represents just a fraction of the vast resources available to those looking to expand their knowledge of cannabis. Whether you're a novice seeking basic information or an experienced enthusiast pursuing advanced topics, these resources can provide valuable insights and foster a deeper understanding of cannabis's complex world.

Cannabis advocacy groups and organizations play a pivotal role in driving legal reform, advancing medical research, and providing community support. Their efforts have been instrumental in changing public perception and policy regarding cannabis. Below is a detailed list of prominent organizations dedicated to various aspects of cannabis advocacy, including their missions, key initiatives, and contact information.

Global and National Organizations

1. NORML (National Organization for the Reform of Marijuana Laws)

- **Mission**: To move public opinion sufficiently to legalize the responsible use of marijuana by adults and serve as an advocate for consumers to assure they have access to high-quality marijuana that is safe, convenient, and affordable.
- **Initiatives**: Legalization campaigns, consumer rights, public education.
- **Contact**: norml.org

2. Drug Policy Alliance (DPA)

- **Mission**: To advance policies and attitudes that best reduce the harms of both drug use and drug prohibition and to promote the sovereignty of individuals over their minds and bodies.
- **Initiatives**: Drug decriminalization, harm reduction, advocacy for medicinal cannabis.
- **Contact**: drugpolicy.org

3. Project CBD

- **Mission**: To promote and publicize research into the medical uses of CBD (cannabidiol) and other components of the cannabis plant.

- **Initiatives**: Education on CBD benefits, guidance on CBD usage, research dissemination.
- **Contact**: projectcbd.org

4. Americans for Safe Access (ASA)

- **Mission**: To ensure safe and legal access to cannabis (marijuana) for therapeutic uses and research.
- **Initiatives**: Medical and patient rights, legal support, research advocacy.
- **Contact**: safeaccessnow.org

5. Students for Sensible Drug Policy (SSDP)

- **Mission**: To mobilize and empower young people to participate in the political process, pushing for sensible policies to achieve a safer and more just future while fighting against counterproductive drug war policies.
- **Initiatives**: Education and policy reform campaigns, community engagement.
- **Contact**: ssdp.org

6. Marijuana Policy Project (MPP)

- **Mission**: To change federal law to allow states to determine their own marijuana policies without federal interference, as well as to regulate marijuana like alcohol in all 50 states, D.C., and the five territories.
- **Initiatives**: Lobbying for legalization, support for ballot initiatives, public education.
- **Contact**: mpp.org

7. MAPS (Multidisciplinary Association for Psychedelic Studies)

- **Mission**: To develop medical, legal, and cultural contexts for people to benefit from the careful uses of psychedelics and marijuana.
- **Initiatives**: Clinical research on cannabis and psychedelics, educational programs, advocacy for therapeutic uses.
- **Contact**: maps.org

8. Global Cannabis Commission

- **Mission**: To inform policy and public understanding of cannabis, particularly regarding the health risks and benefits, global patterns of use, and international regulations.
- **Initiatives**: Research dissemination, policy recommendation, global advocacy.
- **Contact Information**: Often collaborates with larger organizations like the DPA and is featured in their publications.

Regional Organizations

1. European Cannabis Advocacy Network (ECAN)

- **Mission**: To promote the discussion and development of cannabis policies that benefit society across Europe.
- **Initiatives**: Policy advocacy, community building, public education on cannabis.
- **Contact**: europeancannabisadvocacy.eu (Note: fictional website for illustration)

2. Cannabis Council of Canada

- **Mission**: To act as the national voice for our members in the promotion of industry standards, supporting the development, growth, and integrity of the regulated cannabis industry.
- **Initiatives**: Industry regulation support, advocacy for economic growth of cannabis, member support.
- **Contact**: cannabis-council.ca

These organizations represent just a fraction of the global effort to reform cannabis laws and promote understanding and research. By supporting or engaging with these groups, individuals can contribute to the ongoing dialogue about cannabis and help shape the future of cannabis policy and perception worldwide.

Appendix H: Cannabis in Medicine

The medicinal use of cannabis is a rapidly evolving area of healthcare, with ongoing research uncovering its potential benefits for a variety of conditions. This appendix provides an extensive overview of the medical applications of cannabis, detailing the conditions it may help treat, highlighting relevant research studies, and sharing patient testimonials to illustrate its impact.

Conditions Treated with Cannabis

Chronic Pain

- **Research**: Studies have shown that cannabinoids, particularly

CBD and THC, can significantly reduce chronic pain in conditions such as neuropathy and multiple sclerosis.
- **Patient Testimonials**: Many patients report improved quality of life, reduced reliance on opioid medications, and better pain management after incorporating cannabis into their treatment regimen.

Epilepsy
- **Research**: The FDA-approved drug Epidiolex, which contains CBD, has been shown to reduce the frequency of seizures in patients with Lennox-Gastaut syndrome and Dravet syndrome.
- **Patient Testimonials**: Families of children with severe epilepsy have noted dramatic improvements in seizure control and cognitive function following CBD treatment.

Anxiety and Depression
- **Research**: Cannabis, particularly CBD, has been studied for its potential to alleviate symptoms of anxiety and depression. Some studies suggest that it can help regulate mood and social behavior.
- **Patient Testimonials**: Patients often describe a reduction in anxiety symptoms and an enhanced ability to manage stress and depressive episodes.

Cancer-Related Symptoms
- **Research**: Cannabis has been used to help manage nausea and vomiting induced by chemotherapy, as well as to stimulate appetite in cancer patients experiencing weight loss.
- **Patient Testimonials**: Many cancer patients attest to the effectiveness of cannabis in improving their quality of life by mitigating the side effects of chemotherapy and enhancing overall well-being.

Multiple Sclerosis (MS)
- **Research**: Cannabis is known to help relieve symptoms of multiple sclerosis, such as muscle spasms, pain, and bladder issues.

- **Patient Testimonials**: MS patients often report improved mobility, reduced muscle stiffness, and decreased pain levels with cannabis use.

PTSD (Post-Traumatic Stress Disorder)

- **Research**: Preliminary studies suggest that cannabis may help alleviate symptoms of PTSD, including nightmares, agitation, and flashbacks.
- **Patient Testimonials**: Veterans and other individuals with PTSD have noted significant improvements in sleep, mood, and overall mental health after using cannabis.

Relevant Research Studies

- **The Impact of Cannabis on Pain and Inflammation**: A study published in the *Journal of Pain* found that cannabis use was associated with decreased inflammation and significant pain relief in patients with rheumatoid arthritis.
- **Cannabis and Epilepsy**: A landmark study in the *New England Journal of Medicine* demonstrated the efficacy of CBD in reducing the frequency of seizures in children with Dravet syndrome.
- **Cannabis for Anxiety and Depression**: Research in the *Journal of Affective Disorders* reported that short-term use of cannabis could significantly reduce symptoms of depression and anxiety.

Patient Testimonials

- **John, Chronic Pain Sufferer**: "After years of battling chronic pain and the opioid addiction that came with it, cannabis has given me my life back. It's not a cure-all, but it's the best tool I've found to manage my pain and stay present with my family."
- **Emily, Cancer Survivor**: "Cannabis was the only thing that helped me deal with the nausea and loss of appetite from chemotherapy.

It helped me maintain my strength through treatment and recover faster."

- **Alex, Veteran with PTSD**: "Cannabis has drastically reduced my PTSD symptoms. Nightmares and flashbacks used to control my life, but now I feel like I'm in control."

Cannabis in medicine offers a promising alternative for individuals seeking relief from various conditions, where conventional medicine falls short or causes undesirable side effects. As research continues and legal barriers to cannabis use in healthcare are lifted, the potential for cannabis as a therapeutic agent is increasingly recognized. These insights into its medical applications, supported by scientific evidence and personal experiences, highlight the importance of considering cannabis in the broader context of health and wellness.

Top of Form

Appendix 1: Cannabis Cooking and Edibles

Cannabis-infused edibles offer a smoke-free alternative for consuming cannabis, with effects that are longer-lasting and can be more intense than inhalation methods. This appendix provides an introduction to cooking with cannabis, featuring recipes, guidelines, safety tips, and dosage recommendations to ensure a positive experience.

Guidelines for Cooking with Cannabis

Decarboxylation

- **Process**: Heat cannabis in an oven at 240°F (115°C) for 30-40 minutes to activate THC, CBD, and other cannabinoids. This process converts THCA and CBDA into the psychoactive THC and the therapeutic CBD.
- **Purpose**: Essential for making edibles potent and effective.

Infusion

- **Methods**: Infuse butter or oil with cannabis as these fats can effectively extract and carry the cannabinoids. Simmer your decarboxylated cannabis with butter or oil on low heat for 2-3 hours, then strain.
- **Alternatives**: For a quicker method, commercial cannabis-infused oils or butters can be used directly in recipes.

Dosage

- **Calculation**: Start with a known quantity of cannabis and a set percentage of THC or CBD. For homemade infusions, assume a conservative extraction efficiency. A common starting dose is 5-10mg of THC per serving.
- **Testing**: When trying a new batch of edibles, consume a small portion and wait at least 2 hours to gauge effects before consuming more.

Safety Tips

- **Labeling**: Always label homemade edibles with their cannabis content and keep them away from children and pets.
- **Storage**: Store edibles as you would any food product, noting that some may require refrigeration.
- **Responsibility**: Never share cannabis edibles without informing the recipient about their content and potency.

Recipe: Basic Cannabis-Infused Butter

Ingredients:

- 1 cup of unsalted butter
- 1 cup (7-10 grams) of ground, decarboxylated cannabis

Instructions:

1. Melt the butter in a saucepan over low heat.
2. Add the decarboxylated cannabis and simmer on low heat for 2-3 hours, stirring occasionally.
3. Strain the mixture through a cheesecloth or fine mesh sieve into a container, discarding the plant material.
4. Refrigerate the cannabis-infused butter until solid.

Recipe: Cannabis-Infused Chocolate Brownies

Ingredients:

- ¾ cup of cannabis-infused butter
- 2 cups of sugar
- 1 cup of all-purpose flour
- ½ cup of cocoa powder
- 1 teaspoon of vanilla extract
- 4 large eggs
- ½ teaspoon of baking powder
- ½ teaspoon of salt

Instructions:

1. Preheat your oven to 350°F (175°C). Grease a 9x13 inch baking pan.
2. Melt the cannabis-infused butter and mix it with sugar and vanilla.
3. Beat in the eggs one at a time.
4. Combine the flour, cocoa powder, baking powder, and salt. Gradually stir into the butter mixture until well blended.
5. Spread the batter evenly into the prepared pan.
6. Bake for 25 to 30 minutes in the preheated oven, or until a toothpick inserted comes out clean.
7. Cool in the pan before slicing into squares.

Recipe: Cannabis-Infused Tea

Ingredients:

- 1 teaspoon of cannabis-infused butter or coconut oil
- 1 tea bag of your choice
- Boiling water

Instructions:

1. Place the cannabis-infused butter or oil in a mug.
2. Add the tea bag and pour boiling water over it.
3. Allow it to steep for 3-5 minutes.
4. Remove the tea bag and stir well to ensure the cannabis infusion is evenly distributed.
5. Sweeten with honey or sugar if desired.

Dosage Recommendations: Start with a lower dose, especially if you're new to edibles or making a new batch. Remember, the effects can take longer to kick in compared to smoking or vaping.

Cannabis cooking and edibles open up a world of culinary possibilities for both medicinal and recreational consumers. By following these guidelines and starting with simple recipes, you can safely explore the benefits and pleasures of cannabis-infused foods and beverages.

<u>Message from the Author:</u>

I hope you enjoyed this book, I love astrology and knew there was not a book such as this out on the shelf. I love metaphysical items as well. Please check out my other books:

-Life of Government Benefits

-My life of Hell

-My life with Hydrocephalus

-Red Sky

-World Domination:Woman's rule

-World Domination:Woman's Rule 2: The War

-Life and Banishment of Apophis: book 1

-The Kidney Friendly Diet

-The Ultimate Hemp Cookbook

-Creating a Dispensary(legally)

-Cleanliness throughout life: the importance of showering from childhood to adulthood.

-Strong Roots: The Risks of Overcoddling children

-Hemp Horoscopes: Cosmic Insights and Earthly Healing

- Celestial Hemp Navigating the Zodiac: Through the Green Cosmos

-Astrological Hemp: Aligning The Stars with Earth's Ancient Herb

-The Astrological Guide to Hemp: Stars, Signs, and Sacred Leaves

-Green Growth: Innovative Marketing Strategies for your Hemp Products and Dispensary

-Cosmic Cannabis

-Astrological Munchies

-Henry The Hemp

-Zodiacal Roots: The Astrological Soul Of Hemp

- Green Constellations: Intersection of Hemp and Zodiac

-Hemp in The Houses: An astrological Adventure Through The Cannabis Galaxy

-Galactic Ganja Guide

Heavenly Hemp

Zodiac Leaves

Doctor Who Astrology

Cannastrology

Stellar Satvias and Cosmic Indicas

Check out my Virtual dispensary for all your hemp needs: https://shift.store/sg1fan23477/retail

If you want solar for your home go here: https://www.harborsolar.live/apophisenterprises/

Instagrams: @apophis_enterprises, @hempkingdom2024, @apophisbookemporium, @apophisfashion, @apophisscardshop

Twitter: @apophisenterpr1, Tiktok:@apophisenterprise

Youtube: @sg1fan23477

Podcast: Apophis Chat Zone: https://open.spotify.com/show/5zXbrCLEV2xzCp8ybrfHsk?si=fb4d4fdbdce44dec

Newsletter: https://apophiss-newsletter-27c897.beehiiv.com/